EMMANUEL JOSEPH

Academic Excellence: Strategies for College and University Success

Contents

1

Chapter 1: Introduction to Effective Study Methods

S tudying effectively is a fundamental skill that can make a world of difference in your academic journey. This chapter serves as a foundational introduction to the best study methods for college and university students, highlighting the importance of cultivating good study habits and setting the stage for success.

1.1 The Importance of Effective Study Methods

Successful academic achievement is not solely about innate intelligence; it largely depends on how effectively you can absorb, retain, and apply knowledge. Effective study methods are the key to unlocking your full academic potential. They are the tools that bridge the gap between merely going through the motions of studying and truly understanding and mastering your subjects.

1.2 Setting Realistic Expectations

Before delving into specific study techniques, it's essential to set realistic expectations. While achieving A's is a noble goal, it's also important to acknowledge that academic performance varies among individuals, and not every subject may come naturally to you. The aim of effective study methods is to help you perform to the best of your abilities, whatever that level may be. Consistent effort and smart strategies are more valuable than expecting perfection in every subject.

1.3 The Role of Discipline

Effective studying requires discipline and consistency. It's about creating a structured routine and adhering to it. This doesn't mean you have to study for long, grueling hours each day. Rather, it means dedicating focused, uninterrupted time to your studies. This discipline will help you stay organized, meet deadlines, and ultimately reduce stress.

1.4 The Power of Good Study Habits

Good study habits are the building blocks of effective study methods. Habits such as time management, organization, setting goals, and maintaining a conducive study environment are the framework upon which you can build successful academic performance. Throughout this guide, we will explore these habits in detail and provide practical strategies for incorporating them into your routine.

1.5 A Holistic Approach to Learning

Effective study methods encompass not just what you do when you sit down with your textbooks but also how you approach your entire learning experience. This includes finding your unique learning style, seeking support when needed, and adopting a growth mindset that encourages continuous improvement.

1.6 Chapter Summary

In this introductory chapter, we've outlined the overarching principles of effective study methods for college and university students. You've learned that studying effectively is not just about the techniques you use but also about setting realistic expectations, maintaining discipline, and fostering good study habits.

The subsequent chapters in this guide will delve into specific strategies and techniques to help you excel in your studies. Whether you're striving for A's in your courses or simply aiming to reach your full academic potential, these chapters will provide you with valuable insights and actionable steps to enhance your learning experience.

2

Chapter 2: Time Management

T ime management is a critical aspect of effective study methods for college and university students. This chapter explores strategies for managing your time efficiently, creating a study schedule, and ensuring that you make the most of your available time.

2.1 The Value of Time

Time is a finite resource, and as a student, you likely have multiple commitments, including classes, assignments, extracurricular activities, and possibly part-time work. To succeed academically, it's crucial to recognize the value of your time and make the most of it.

2.2 Setting Priorities

Effective time management begins with setting priorities. Determine which tasks and activities are most important in your academic and personal life. This might involve identifying key assignments, upcoming exams, and personal goals.

2.3 Creating a Study Schedule

A well-structured study schedule can help you allocate sufficient time to various subjects and assignments. Consider the following when creating your schedule:

- Time blocks: Allocate specific blocks of time for studying each subject.
   - Consistency: Maintain a regular study routine to establish a sense of discipline.
   - Flexibility: Adapt your schedule as needed to accommodate changes in your workload.

2.4 Eliminating Time Wasters

Identify common time-wasting habits and strive to eliminate them. This includes reducing distractions, such as excessive social media use or procrastination. Implement techniques like the Pomodoro method, which involves focused work periods followed by short breaks, to enhance your productivity.

2.5 Avoiding Overcommitment

While extracurricular activities and part-time jobs can be valuable, overcommitting yourself can lead to burnout and hinder your academic performance. Strike a balance between your academic and non-academic commitments.

2.6 Using Time Management Tools

Consider utilizing time management tools and techniques. These might include digital calendars, to-do lists, and apps designed to help you stay organized and on track.

2.7 Time for Self-Care

Time management isn't just about studying—it should also account for time to relax and engage in self-care activities. Adequate sleep, exercise, and time with friends and family are essential for maintaining your physical and mental well-being.

2.8 Chapter Summary

This chapter has explored the vital role of time management in effective study methods. By understanding the value of your time, setting priorities, creating a study schedule, eliminating time wasters, and finding a balance between academic and personal life, you can make the most of your time and boost your academic performance.

Effective time management is the cornerstone of academic success, providing you with the structure and discipline needed to excel in your studies. In the subsequent chapters of this guide, we will delve deeper into specific study techniques that align with your well-organized schedule.

3

Chapter 3: Goal Setting

Setting clear and achievable academic goals is a fundamental component of effective study methods. This chapter explores the significance of goal setting in your academic journey and provides strategies for defining and pursuing your goals.

3.1 The Power of Goals

Goals give your academic journey direction and purpose. They serve as motivational milestones, guiding your efforts and providing a sense of achievement as you progress. Without clear goals, your study methods may lack focus and purpose.

3.2 Types of Academic Goals

Academic goals can be categorized into two main types:

- Short-term goals: These are specific, achievable objectives that you aim to accomplish within a relatively short time frame, such as completing an assignment or mastering a particular topic.

- Long-term goals: These are broader, more comprehensive goals that encompass your overall academic aspirations, like achieving a certain GPA, graduating with honors, or pursuing a specific career path.

3.3 SMART Goal Setting

One effective approach to goal setting is using the SMART criteria:

- Specific: Goals should be well-defined and precise.
   - Measurable: You should be able to track your progress and determine when you've achieved the goal.
   - Achievable: Goals should be realistic and within your capabilities.
   - Relevant: Goals should align with your academic and personal aspirations.
   - Time-bound: Establish a clear time frame for achieving your goals.

3.4 Creating a Goal Plan

Develop a written goal plan that includes your short-term and long-term goals. This plan can serve as a roadmap for your academic journey. Include specific steps, milestones, and deadlines for each goal.

3.5 Tracking Progress

Regularly review and update your goals and track your progress. This allows you to make necessary adjustments and stay on the path to achievement. Tools such as goal-tracking apps or a journal can help with this process.

3.6 Overcoming Challenges

Goal setting isn't always straightforward. You may encounter obstacles or setbacks. In this chapter, you'll also learn about strategies for overcoming challenges and staying motivated when pursuing your goals.

3.7 Chapter Summary

In this chapter, you've explored the importance of setting academic goals and how to do it effectively. Goal setting provides you with a clear sense of purpose, motivation, and a structured plan for your academic journey.

As you move forward in your studies, remember to set SMART goals, create a goal plan, and regularly track your progress. In the subsequent chapters of this guide, we'll dive into specific study techniques that will help you achieve these goals and excel academically.

4

Chapter 4: Active Learning Techniques

Active learning is a dynamic and engaging approach to studying that involves interacting with the material, rather than passively absorbing it. In this chapter, we will explore various active learning techniques that can enhance your understanding of course material and help you excel academically.

4.1 What Is Active Learning?

Active learning is a pedagogical approach that shifts the responsibility for learning from the instructor to the student. It encourages students to participate in the learning process actively, fostering higher levels of engagement and understanding.

4.2 Benefits of Active Learning

Active learning techniques have numerous advantages:

- Improved retention: Active learning promotes better memory retention and recall.
    - Enhanced understanding: Engaging with the material leads to a deeper understanding.

- Critical thinking: It encourages students to think critically and apply knowledge.

- Collaboration: Active learning often involves group activities, which can enhance collaboration and communication skills.

4.3 Active Learning Techniques

Several active learning techniques can be incorporated into your study routine:

- Discussion and Debate: Engage in discussions and debates about course topics with peers or through online forums. This helps you think critically and articulate your ideas effectively.

- Concept Mapping: Create visual representations of course material using concept maps. This technique helps you see how different ideas and concepts are interconnected.

- Problem-Solving: Practice solving problems related to your course material. Whether it's math equations, case studies, or scientific experiments, problem-solving is a powerful way to apply what you've learned.

- Teaching Others: Explaining concepts or teaching them to someone else can reinforce your understanding and knowledge.

- Self-Testing: Regularly quiz yourself on course material to reinforce your memory and identify areas that require further study.

- Interactive Note-Taking: Instead of passively transcribing lectures, engage with your notes by adding questions, comments, or personal insights. This active note-taking approach makes your notes more valuable study tools.

- Hands-On Learning: If your course allows, engage in hands-on learning experiences. This can be particularly effective for science, technology, engineering, and mathematics (STEM) subjects.

4.4 Balancing Active Learning with Other Study Methods

While active learning is valuable, it's essential to balance it with other study methods, such as reading and reviewing course materials. Incorporating a variety of techniques based on the type of content and your learning style can be a winning strategy.

4.5 Chapter Summary

Active learning techniques provide an exciting and effective way to engage with your course material actively. In this chapter, you've learned about the benefits of active learning and explored a range of techniques you can incorporate into your study routine.

As you progress in your academic journey, remember that active learning enhances your understanding, critical thinking skills, and collaboration abilities. In the subsequent chapters of this guide, we'll continue to explore more study methods and techniques to help you excel academically.

5

Chapter 5: Finding Your Learning Style

Understanding your unique learning style is a crucial aspect of effective study methods. In this chapter, we'll delve into the concept of learning styles, help you identify your preferred style, and provide strategies for tailoring your study methods to optimize your learning experience.

5.1 What Are Learning Styles?

Learning styles refer to the different ways in which individuals naturally prefer to absorb, process, and retain information. People have diverse learning styles, and recognizing yours can significantly enhance your study methods.

5.2 Common Learning Styles

There are several well-known learning styles, including:

- Visual: Visual learners prefer information presented in the form of images, charts, graphs, and diagrams.

- Auditory: Auditory learners learn best through listening, such as lectures, discussions, and audio materials.

- Kinesthetic/Tactile: Kinesthetic learners thrive when they can engage with material physically, such as through hands-on activities or interactive experiments.

- Reading/Writing: These learners excel when they read and write about course content, taking detailed notes and summarizing key points.

5.3 Identifying Your Learning Style

To identify your learning style, consider your preferences in various learning situations. Reflect on which activities or approaches have helped you grasp and remember information most effectively. You might also find online quizzes and assessments that can provide insights into your learning style.

5.4 Tailoring Your Study Methods

Once you understand your learning style, you can tailor your study methods to align with it. For example:

- Visual learners can benefit from creating colorful, organized study materials, like mind maps or flashcards.

- Auditory learners might find value in recording lectures and listening to them multiple times, or they can participate in group discussions.

- Kinesthetic learners can enhance their understanding by engaging in hands-on activities, conducting experiments, or using physical models.

- Reading/Writing learners should focus on creating written summaries, taking comprehensive notes, and rereading course materials.

5.5 Adapting to Different Learning Styles

While it's essential to cater to your primary learning style, versatility is also valuable. You may encounter different teaching styles and materials that don't align perfectly with your preferred style. Being adaptable and open to different learning experiences can be advantageous.

5.6 Chapter Summary

In this chapter, you've explored the concept of learning styles and how they can influence your study methods. Understanding your learning style empowers you to customize your approach to learning, making your study sessions more effective and enjoyable.

As you continue your academic journey, remember to adapt your study methods to your learning style while remaining open to different experiences. In the subsequent chapters of this guide, we'll delve deeper into specific strategies that align with your unique style, helping you excel academically.

6

Chapter 6: Memorization Techniques

Memorization is a fundamental part of effective study methods. In this chapter, we will explore various techniques and strategies to help you improve your memory retention, allowing you to recall information more effectively for exams and assignments.

6.1 The Importance of Memory

Memory is the foundation of learning. Whether you need to remember facts, dates, equations, or concepts, a strong memory is essential for academic success.

6.2 Understanding How Memory Works

Memory involves three key processes:

- Encoding: This is the process of taking in information and converting it into a form that can be stored in your memory.

- Storage: Once information is encoded, it is stored in your memory system for later retrieval.

- Retrieval: This is the process of accessing stored information when you need it.

6.3 Memorization Techniques

There are several effective memorization techniques you can employ:

- Repetition: Repeating information multiple times can strengthen memory retention. This can involve reading and re-reading notes, flashcards, or key concepts.

- Mnemonic Devices: Mnemonics are memory aids that make it easier to recall information. Examples include acronyms, visual imagery, and rhymes.

- Chunking: Divide complex information into smaller, manageable chunks. For example, instead of trying to memorize a long string of numbers, break them into groups.

- Visualization: Create mental images or mind maps to help you visualize and connect information. This technique is particularly useful for remembering processes and sequences.

- Spaced Repetition: This technique involves revisiting information at increasing intervals. Over time, this reinforces memory and enhances long-term retention.

- Active Recall: Test yourself by recalling information without looking at your notes or textbooks. This technique challenges your memory and strengthens it.

- Interleaved Practice: Instead of studying one topic at a time, mix subjects or topics. This technique boosts memory retention and aids in distinguishing between different concepts.

6.4 Study Environment and Mindset

Creating a conducive study environment and having the right mindset are also important for effective memorization. Minimize distractions, ensure adequate sleep, and stay motivated. Anxiety and stress can hinder memory, so practicing stress-reduction techniques can be valuable.

6.5 Chapter Summary

In this chapter, you've explored the significance of memory in your academic journey and learned various techniques to enhance memory retention. Effective memorization techniques can help you remember information more efficiently, ultimately leading to improved exam performance and coursework comprehension.

As you continue your studies, practice these memorization techniques, adapt them to your learning style, and incorporate them into your study routine. In the subsequent chapters of this guide, we'll delve deeper into strategies for reading, note-taking, and test preparation to further enhance your academic performance.

7

Chapter 7: Reading Strategies

Reading is a fundamental part of your academic journey, and it's essential to have effective strategies for comprehending and retaining the material. In this chapter, we'll explore strategies for reading textbooks, academic papers, and other course-related materials more efficiently.

7.1 The Importance of Effective Reading

Reading is a primary means of acquiring knowledge and understanding complex subject matter. Effective reading strategies are crucial for success in college and university courses.

7.2 Before You Start Reading

Before diving into your reading material, consider these preparatory steps:

- Preview the Material: Quickly scan the material to get an overview of its content. Read headings, subheadings, and any summary sections. This preview primes your mind for what's to come.

- Set a Purpose: Determine why you're reading the material. Are you looking for specific information, seeking an overall understanding, or studying for an exam? Setting a clear purpose can guide your reading.

7.3 Active Reading Strategies

Active reading techniques engage your mind and help you retain information more effectively:

- Highlighting and Note-Taking: While reading, use highlighting, underlining, and margin notes to mark key points, definitions, and insights. This process helps you engage with the material actively and provides a valuable reference for later review.

- Annotating: Annotating involves making comments or questions in the margins of the text. This encourages critical thinking and a deeper understanding of the material.

- Summarizing: After reading a section, take a moment to summarize what you've learned in your own words. This solidifies your comprehension and helps you remember key points.

- Questioning: As you read, ask questions about the material. This encourages a more active and inquisitive approach to learning.

7.4 Effective Note-Taking While Reading

Taking notes while reading is a critical skill:

- Organize your notes by topic or chapter.
    - Use shorthand and abbreviations to save time.
    - Create a system for highlighting and annotating your notes to make important points stand out.

7.5 Speed Reading Techniques

For dense reading materials or when you have limited time, speed reading techniques can be valuable. These include techniques like using a pointer (e.g., your finger) to guide your eyes, reducing subvocalization (the habit of silently saying words as you read), and practicing skimming and scanning.

7.6 Chapter Summary

In this chapter, you've learned about the importance of effective reading strategies in your academic journey. These strategies, such as active reading, annotating, summarizing, and questioning, help you engage with the material actively and enhance your comprehension and retention of course content.

As you continue your studies, incorporate these reading strategies into your routine, adapt them to your learning style, and apply them to various types of academic materials. In the subsequent chapters of this guide, we'll explore techniques for test preparation, effective note-taking, and managing test anxiety to further boost your academic performance.

8

Chapter 8: Test Preparation and Test-Taking Strategies

Success in college and university often hinges on how well you prepare for and perform on exams. In this chapter, we will explore strategies for effective test preparation and test-taking that can help you excel in your assessments.

8.1 The Importance of Test Preparation

Effective test preparation is crucial because it ensures you're ready to demonstrate your understanding of the material. Proper preparation can reduce stress and increase your chances of success.

8.2 Test Preparation Strategies

- Organize Your Study Materials: Gather all the materials you need to study, including textbooks, notes, and resources. Create a clean and organized workspace.

- Review Your Notes: Go through your class notes, highlighting key points and summarizing the main concepts.

- Practice Active Recall: Test yourself on the material to reinforce your memory. Use flashcards, quizzes, or create your own practice questions.

- Prioritize Weak Areas: Identify areas where you struggle and spend more time studying them.

- Use Review Guides and Study Aids: Many textbooks have review sections or study guides at the end of chapters. Take advantage of these resources.

- Group Study: Collaborate with peers to discuss and quiz each other on the material. Group study can provide diverse insights and encourage active learning.

8.3 Test-Taking Strategies

- Read Instructions Carefully: Before starting the exam, thoroughly read the instructions and ensure you understand the format and requirements.

- Budget Your Time: Divide your available time among the exam questions or sections, ensuring you have enough time to complete the entire test.

- Start with What You Know: Begin with the questions you are most confident about. This builds your confidence and ensures you don't miss out on easy points.

- Answer Every Question: Even if you're unsure about an answer, provide your best guess. In most cases, it's better to take a chance rather than leave questions blank.

- Manage Stress and Stay Calm: Use stress-reduction techniques, like deep breathing or mindfulness, to stay calm during the exam.

- Review Your Work: If time allows, go back and review your answers. Check for errors and ensure you've answered all questions.

8.4 Types of Tests

Different types of tests (e.g., multiple-choice, essay, short answer) require distinct strategies. Familiarize yourself with the types of tests you'll encounter in your courses and prepare accordingly.

8.5 Post-Test Review

After taking an exam, review your performance. Identify areas where you did well and areas where you need improvement. Use this feedback to adjust your study methods for future assessments.

8.6 Chapter Summary

In this chapter, you've learned about the importance of effective test preparation and test-taking strategies. Proper preparation, active recall, time management, and stress reduction are essential components of successful test performance.

As you continue your academic journey, remember to adapt these strategies to different types of exams and continue refining your test preparation and test-taking skills. In the subsequent chapters of this guide, we'll explore other aspects of academic success, including note-taking, time management, and stress management.

9

Chapter 9: Study Groups and Collaborative Learning

S tudy groups and collaborative learning can be powerful tools to enhance your academic success in college and university. In this chapter, we'll explore the benefits of studying with others and provide tips for effectively participating in study groups.

9.1 The Power of Study Groups

Study groups and collaborative learning offer several advantages:

- Diverse Perspectives: Study groups bring together students with different backgrounds and viewpoints, enriching your understanding of the material.

- Active Engagement: Engaging in discussions, debates, and teaching others can reinforce your own knowledge and improve comprehension.

- Accountability: Study groups help you stay accountable to a study schedule and ensure you're on track with the material.

- Social Support: Collaborative learning can reduce the isolation often associated with intense studying, fostering a sense of community and support.

9.2 Finding or Forming a Study Group

Here's how to find or create a study group:

- Classmates: Start by connecting with your classmates and identifying those interested in forming a study group. You can do this through class announcements, social media, or in-person discussions.

- Library or Study Areas: Study groups often form in common study areas or libraries. You can look for or create a group in these locations.

- Online Platforms: Consider using online platforms or social media groups to find or form virtual study groups, especially if your classmates are spread out geographically.

9.3 Effective Study Group Dynamics

To make the most of your study group, consider these dynamics:

- Leadership Roles: Assign specific roles within the group, such as a discussion leader, timekeeper, or note-taker, to ensure meetings are productive.

- Structured Meetings: Plan and structure study group meetings with a clear agenda. Focus on specific topics or assignments.

- Active Participation: Encourage active participation from all members. Share your insights and ask questions to foster discussion.

- Review and Summarize: As a group, review and summarize key course concepts, share notes, and teach one another.

- Discussion and Clarification: Use study groups for discussing challenging topics, clarifying doubts, and gaining alternative perspectives.

9.4 Balancing Social and Study Time

While study groups can provide social support, it's important to strike a balance between socializing and studying. Clearly define the purpose of each meeting and allocate time for productive study sessions.

9.5 Chapter Summary

In this chapter, you've learned about the benefits of study groups and collaborative learning in your academic journey. Study groups offer diverse perspectives, active engagement, accountability, and social support.

As you engage in study groups, remember to structure your meetings effectively, actively participate, and balance social interactions with productive study sessions. In the subsequent chapters of this guide, we'll continue to explore strategies and techniques to help you excel academically.

10

Chapter 10: Avoiding Procrastination

Procrastination is a common challenge for students, but overcoming it is essential for academic success. In this chapter, we'll explore strategies to identify, manage, and overcome procrastination, helping you stay on track with your studies.

10.1 Understanding Procrastination

Procrastination is the act of delaying tasks or activities, often in favor of less important or more enjoyable ones. It can be a significant barrier to effective studying and time management.

10.2 Common Causes of Procrastination

Identifying the root causes of procrastination can help you address the issue effectively. Common causes include:

- Lack of motivation
    - Fear of failure
    - Feeling overwhelmed
    - Poor time management
    - Perfectionism

10.3 Strategies to Overcome Procrastination

Here are some effective strategies to help you combat procrastination:

- Set Clear Goals: Clearly define your goals and the tasks required to achieve them. This clarity can boost motivation.

- Break Tasks into Smaller Steps: Divide large or complex tasks into smaller, more manageable steps. This can make the work seem less intimidating.

- Use Time Management Techniques: Techniques like the Pomodoro method, time blocking, and to-do lists can help structure your study time.

- Find Your Peak Productivity Time: Identify the time of day when you are most alert and productive, and schedule your most challenging tasks during that period.

- Minimize Distractions: Create a distraction-free study environment. Turn off or silence your phone, block distracting websites, and let friends and family know your study hours.

- Reward Yourself: Set up a system of rewards for completing tasks. Treat yourself to something enjoyable after you finish your work.

- Visualize Success: Imagine the satisfaction and sense of accomplishment you'll feel when you complete your tasks. Visualization can be a powerful motivator.

- Seek Accountability: Share your goals with a friend or study partner who can help hold you accountable.

- Practice Self-Compassion: Be kind to yourself and recognize that it's okay to have off days or make mistakes. Avoid self-criticism and self-blame.

10.4 Developing Good Study Habits

Cultivating good study habits, such as maintaining a consistent study routine and staying organized, can prevent procrastination from taking hold.

10.5 Seeking Help for Chronic Procrastination

If you find that procrastination is severely impacting your academic performance and well-being, consider seeking help from a counselor or therapist. Chronic procrastination can sometimes be a sign of underlying issues like anxiety or perfectionism.

10.6 Chapter Summary

In this chapter, you've learned about the common causes of procrastination and effective strategies to overcome it. Procrastination can hinder your academic success, but with the right techniques and habits, you can manage it and stay on track with your studies.

As you work on overcoming procrastination, remember that it's a process. Be patient with yourself and continue to apply these strategies in your academic journey. In the subsequent chapters of this guide, we'll explore further techniques to enhance your academic performance, including stress management and self-care.

11

Chapter 11: Stress Management and Self-Care

anaging stress and practicing self-care are vital components of effective study methods. In this chapter, we'll explore strategies for coping with academic stress and maintaining your physical and mental well-being.

11.1 The Impact of Stress on Academic Performance

Stress is a common part of college and university life, but when it becomes chronic or overwhelming, it can hinder your academic performance. Understanding the effects of stress is the first step in managing it effectively.

11.2 Identifying Sources of Stress

To manage stress, it's important to identify its sources, which can vary from academic pressures to personal issues. Some common sources of stress for students include:

- Exams and assignments
  - Time management challenges

- Financial concerns
- Personal relationships
- Health issues

11.3 Stress Management Strategies

Here are strategies for managing stress effectively:

- Time Management: Develop a well-organized study schedule and allocate time for relaxation and self-care.

- Stress Reduction Techniques: Practice stress reduction techniques like deep breathing, mindfulness, meditation, and progressive muscle relaxation.

- Physical Activity: Regular exercise can reduce stress, boost mood, and enhance overall well-being.

- Healthy Eating: A balanced diet can provide the energy and nutrients your body needs to cope with stress.

- Sleep: Prioritize sleep to ensure you're well-rested and mentally alert. Lack of sleep can exacerbate stress.

- Social Support: Share your concerns with friends, family, or a counselor. Sometimes, talking about your stress can alleviate its impact.

- Seek Professional Help: If stress becomes overwhelming or leads to mental health issues, consider seeking help from a counselor or therapist.

11.4 Self-Care Practices

Self-care is crucial for maintaining your well-being:

- Relaxation: Set aside time for relaxation activities you enjoy, such as reading, listening to music, or practicing a hobby.

- Balanced Lifestyle: Maintain a balanced lifestyle that includes time for work, study, socializing, and relaxation.

- Self-Compassion: Be kind to yourself and practice self-compassion. Avoid self-criticism and perfectionism.

- Mindfulness and Meditation: These practices can help you stay present and reduce anxiety.

- Limit Technology: Minimize screen time and disconnect from digital devices when possible.

11.5 Chapter Summary

In this chapter, you've explored the impact of stress on academic performance and learned strategies for managing it effectively. Prioritizing self-care and stress management not only supports your academic success but also contributes to your overall well-being.

As you continue your academic journey, remember to integrate these stress management and self-care strategies into your daily routine. By maintaining a balanced and healthy lifestyle, you can enhance your academic performance and enjoy a more fulfilling college or university experience. In the subsequent chapters of this guide, we'll explore further techniques and strategies to excel academically.

12

Chapter 12: Continuous Improvement

Continuous improvement is a fundamental principle in achieving and maintaining academic success. In this final chapter, we'll discuss strategies for self-assessment, seeking academic support, and making ongoing improvements in your study methods.

12.1 The Path to Excellence

Excellence in academics is not a fixed destination but a continuous journey. It involves a commitment to lifelong learning and self-improvement.

12.2 Self-Assessment

Self-assessment is a valuable tool for evaluating your academic progress and identifying areas for improvement. Consider these self-assessment strategies:

- Review your performance in exams, assignments, and coursework.
    - Reflect on your study habits and time management.
    - Identify strengths and weaknesses in specific subjects or areas of study.

12.3 Seeking Academic Support

When you encounter challenges or need additional help, it's essential to know where and how to seek academic support:

- Professors and Instructors: Reach out to your professors or instructors for clarification, guidance, or feedback on your work.

- Academic Advisors: Academic advisors can help you plan your course schedule, choose your major, and navigate academic requirements.

- Tutoring Services: Many institutions offer tutoring services where you can receive one-on-one or group assistance with challenging subjects.

- Study Groups: Collaborate with study groups to gain insights and support from peers.

- Academic Resources: Utilize academic resources, such as libraries, online databases, and writing centers, to enhance your learning.

- Counseling and Mental Health Services: If you're experiencing emotional or mental health challenges that affect your academic performance, consider seeking support from counseling and mental health services.

12.4 Setting New Goals

After self-assessment and seeking academic support, set new goals to target areas for improvement. These goals can encompass:

- Raising your GPA or achieving specific academic honors.
    - Mastering challenging subjects or skills.
    - Enhancing your overall study habits and time management.

12.5 Embracing a Growth Mindset

Cultivate a growth mindset, which emphasizes the belief that abilities and intelligence can be developed through effort and learning. This mindset encourages resilience and a willingness to face challenges as opportunities for growth.

12.6 Lifelong Learning

Commit to lifelong learning, which means continually acquiring new knowledge and skills. Whether through further education, online courses, workshops, or reading, this dedication to learning ensures that your academic journey continues long after your formal studies.

12.7 Chapter Summary

In this final chapter, you've explored the concept of continuous improvement in your academic journey. Self-assessment, seeking academic support, setting new goals, and embracing a growth mindset are all integral to ongoing academic success.

As you continue your studies and move beyond college or university, remember that learning never stops. Embrace new challenges, seek opportunities for growth, and maintain a passion for acquiring knowledge. This dedication to continuous improvement will serve you well throughout your academic and professional life.